MIND CC

GW01451778

Forbidden Manipulation And Deception Techniques To Persuade And Brainwash Anyone

LEONARD MOORE

TABLE OF CONTENTS

FREE BONUS:
3 INSANELY EFFECTIVE WORDS TO
HYPNOTIZE ANYONE IN A CONVERSATION

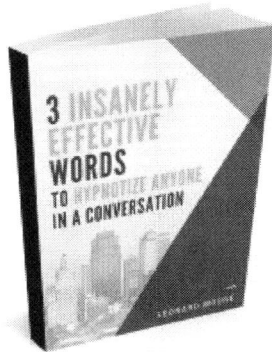

If you're trying to persuade and convince other people then words are the most important tool you absolutely have to master.

As humans we interact with words, we shape the way we think through words, we express ourselves through words. Words evoke feelings and have the ability to talk to the listener's subconscious.

In this free guide you'll discover 3 insanely effective words that you can easily use to start hypnotizing anyone in a conversation.

Go to **www.eepurl.com/cRTY5X** to download the free guide

INTRODUCTION

Thank you for purchasing *Mind Control: Forbidden Manipulation and Deception Techniques to Persuade and Brainwash Anyone*.

This guidebook is going to teach you all about mind control and how you can employ this technique in your life. Using the skills of manipulation, deception and persuasion, you will learn how you can ultimately control your life to create whatever outcome you desire. You will no longer have to stand behind the fear of not getting other people to cooperate with you in order to help you get your desired outcomes because you will be able to subliminally control them without them ever finding out.

This book will teach you about the processes of manipulation, deception, persuasion, mind control, and other incredible NLP techniques. You will also learn about how you can protect yourself from getting caught, and guard yourself from being duped by mind control that is being done unto you by others.

When you are done reading *Mind Control: Forbidden Manipulation and Deception Techniques to Persuade and Brainwash Anyone*, you will be equipped with all of the tools and skills you need in order to generate success with your mind control techniques. This book is aimed for anyone at any level, regardless of how much or how little history you have with mind control techniques. Everyone is sure to learn something from this powerful book, and you will be able to master it as well. This book is designed to help you tap into these forbidden skills and generate great amounts of success in your life as a result.

Some people say getting your way requires effort and hard work on your behalf, but this isn't exactly true. Instead, you can use mind control techniques and get everyone else to do the hard work for you, while you simply sit at the top and profit. You can bring anything into your life and create any outcome you desire with these powerful techniques. Nothing is out of your abilities when you employ mind control and take reality into your own hands.

If you are ready to become the master of your own life and create powerful changes to your reality with minimal effort on your behalf, then read on. Each chapter has been specially designed to help you tap into various areas of mind control and truly master the skill. By the end, you will have everything you need in order to generate major results in your life using mind control strategies. Enjoy!

MIND CONTROL

CHAPTER 1
MIND CONTROL

Mind control is a technique whereby you use various psychological techniques to alter someone's mind. In doing so, you can change the way they think about various things so that their thought processes work in your favor. This technique can enable you to achieve virtually anything you want with the help of virtually anyone you want. It truly puts you in the driver's seat of reality and allows you to have an effortless ability to live your desired life with your desired outcomes.

The History of Mind Control

Mind control has a massive history in society. There are many parts of human history where mind control was used to create desired outcomes. It has been used to assist in exorcisms, possession, and healing mental illnesses in the past.

One of the earliest known forms of mind control was a technique called trephining. This technique involves a tactic where a hole was cut into the skull of a person who was believed to be possessed by evil spirits. It was believed that by cutting the skull open, the hole would enable evil spirits to leave the body. In various parts of the world, an instrument was pushed into the hole to "scare" the spirit away. This technique is essentially the earliest form of a lobotomy. Trephining was believed to be done all around the world as there have been many skulls uncovered from various areas of ancient civilization that feature holes on the cranium.

While you won't be using any physical or harmful tactics on the people you are going to brainwash, it is important to understand the lengthy history of mind control and the fact that it has always been a rather major part of society. In the days of trephining, it was believed that mind control could be accomplished by physical tactics. Essentially, those cutting into the skull believed they could regain control over the mind and have their patient forcefully adopt new ways of thinking and behaving that would be more appropriate to their society.

The idea of possession carried on for centuries, and various types of exorcisms have been completed in those times. Exorcism appears to be one of the primary methods whereby we see mind control, because as we now know, it is not possible for a human to be possessed by a demonic spirit. However, back in those times it was believed to be possible and so individuals would be subjected to brainwashing techniques to attempt to redeem their spirit and return their purity to them. In modern ages, we can suspect that most of these individuals were actually those dealing with mental illness and this was the best way that the society knew how to handle the situation at the time.

As a result of these beliefs, there have been many mind control strategies enforced over the centuries. Straitjackets, shock treatment, seclusion and sensory deprivation, rush chairs, restraining chairs, rotating chairs, and tranquilizing chairs were all some of the more harmful strategies that were enforced as an attempt to brainwash these individuals and return them to normal standards of thinking and behaving. Of course, these days very few of these strategies are used any longer, and there are many statutes of limitations on how the ones that are still used can actually be used.

Furthermore, you don't want to be using any of these in your own brainwashing strategies because they likely won't work.

However, there is one strategy that was developed in history and has been a widely popular form of mind control over the ages. This strategy is still used today, and is even used by many professionals as a means to brainwash patients into a new mindset. This strategy is known as hypnosis. Hypnosis will be a large part of what we use throughout this book, however it won't be the only one. In the remaining portions of this chapter, you will learn about various methods of mind control and how you can employ them to brainwash people into believing what you want them to believe and thus behaving the way you want them to behave.

Dark Psychology

The human condition related to the psychodynamics of those who prey upon others in a way that is motivated by deviant methods is known as dark psychology. Throughout this book you are going to be studying bits of dark psychology because it can help you further understand mind control and how it works.

Virtually every human has the ability to tap into dark psychology. This may sound somewhat terrifying, since dark psychology is often known to be the psychology fostered by psychopaths and sociopaths, and it can be the entire foundation for how many major crimes are committed. However, in this book you are going to learn about dark psychology and how you can use it to your benefit without compromising your own wellbeing, as well as how you can use the understanding of dark psychology to prevent yourself from being brainwashed by others.

The majority of dark psychology is based in goal-oriented motivation that can be rationalized by the individual who is completing the activities. Dark psychology includes the thoughts, feelings, and perceptions fostered by those who are responsible for using dark psychology to complete certain actions.

A lot of the forms of mind control are considered to be rooted in dark psychology because many believe that mind control is an impure strategy used by those who cannot be bothered to do things themselves. They believe that it is a form of evil, hence why it is called "dark" psychology. While we certainly do not want to alleviate the blame from true criminals, you should understand that you are not a criminal for using mind control strategies.

Mind control in this day and age can be a powerful way to encourage people to do the things you need or want them to do. Obviously, this type of powerful strategy can be used to have people do bad things or to create criminal results, but it can also be used to encourage positive results. The way this method works for you is entirely up to you. If you choose to use these strategies to justify and execute criminal behaviors, then you are going to become a criminal and you will likely end up prosecuted as such.

However, if you use these strategies to benefit yourself and those around you without doing harm unto anyone, then there truly is nothing wrong with using mind control to get what you want. There are many people who use mind control for various purposes, such as selling, building businesses, encouraging employees to do what they should be doing in order to keep a business running well, encouraging people to see past their fears and limitations, and much more. Being able to control someone's mind leaves you with a lot of power to do many positive things. Just as much power as you have to do evil things, even. How you choose to use your skillset is entirely up to you.

Various Techniques of Mind Control in Society

In this day and age, there are ten versions of mind control that exist. These are essentially modern-day versions of the techniques you learned about in the "history of mind control" section. Understanding these strategies and how they work will assist you in understanding how they contribute to mind control. After, you will learn about strategies you can employ, and how they work as well!

Education

By educating impressionable children, society essentially teaches them to become "ideal" members of society. They are taught and trained in certain ways that fulfil the desires of the government and authorities, and most people don't even think twice about it.

Advertising and Propaganda

By putting advertising and propaganda everywhere, those in control are capable of eliminating people's feeling of self-worth and encourage them to *need* what is being sold, as opposed to just wanting it. This is essentially a subliminal strategy to make people feel poorly about themselves so that they will purchase whatever is being advertised to increase their feelings of self-worth.

Predictive Programming

The idea of predictive programming is essentially that authorities place references to major activities in the popular media before the atrocity ever takes place. As a result, everyone already warmed up to the idea, and so they are not overly fearful when it takes place. It is essentially a foreshadowing tactic used on real humans, instead of in writing.

Sports, Politics, Religion

The idea of these strategies is to "divide and conquer". Ultimately, each one has people placed into various categories, where they feel very strongly. As a result, they don't come together and support one another, but rather they are against each other. This means that they are divided, and so the authority can conquer.

Food, Water, Air

Believe it or not, there are many toxins and additives that are put into food, water, and air that are literally changing the makeup of your brain. As a result, you are being subjected to mind control every time you consume anything that is essential to your livelihood.

Drugs

Whether they are street drugs or pharmaceutical drugs, they have the ability to alter your brain's chemicals and therefore change your mind. Drugs can be considered akin to old-time lobotomies, shock chairs, and other types of mind control to eliminate mental illness from people. Only, these days, they are much more commonly accepted and are taken by people everywhere.

Military Testing

The military has tested mind control for a long time, claiming that they want to use it as an opportunity to control the opponent and ward off any violence. They have even discussed creating helmets that would protect the militia from mind control strategies and keep them focused on their missions.

Electromagnetic Spectrum

This essentially means the electromagnetic rays that are

cast by electronic devices. We all have our houses filled with them, and every time you plug them in or use them you are subjected to the electromagnetic spectrum. It is believed that this can have a mind-altering effect that would contribute to mind control.

Television, Computer, "Flicker Rate"

Televisions and computers are believed to subject people to overwhelming amounts of information and ideas that ultimately causes them to be hypnotized by the ideas and lulls the information into their subconscious minds, thus creating a situation of mind control. There are also "flicker rates" which means essentially that data is flickering by faster than the eye can see. It is believed that these strategies, including video games, are used to execute mind control strategies.

Nanobots

These are ultimately placed into your brain and used to alter your mind. They believe that by putting a nanobot into your brain they can create any outcome they desire because you are under mind control. You can literally "press a button and become happy".

Understanding the various forms of mind control can help show you the many ways it can be done. While some of these may be chalked up to conspiracy theories, you can still derive a general understanding of how each strategy would contribute to mind control. When you are learning to master mind control, it is important that you understand all of the different ways it can take place.

In the above scenarios, there were some common trends. The general ones included: subliminal messages, mental overwhelm, education, and direct physical altering of the mind. These are the most common methods used to attempt to brainwash someone and control their mind. Some of these strategies are not really doable for the average person, however understanding them will help you later when it comes to preventing yourself from being subject to mind control.

In the meantime, we are going to focus on three primary methods of mind control that you *can* use and easily execute on virtually anyone. They include: persuasion, manipulation, and deception. These methods are all strategies that are completed using spoken word, and they can assist you in altering someone's mind so that you can have your desired effect on them. Now, you will learn about each one.

Persuasion

Persuasion is one of the most popular forms of mind control. This method is used in so many different areas of life that many people don't even recognize when it is happening. That is exactly why it works.

Persuasion is not the same as convincing, although most people believe the two are the same thing. However, persuasion is the act of skillfully encouraging someone to do what you want them to do without them realizing you're doing it, whereas convincing someone means that you are using tactics that are easy to recognize. To explain it a bit further, persuading means to skillfully present facts and information in a way that doesn't make it obvious that you are doing so, and encouraging people to do what you desire for them to do. Convincing people, on the other hand, is very obvious and often includes a lot of back-and-forth and ultimately nagging, begging, or pleading someone to make the decision you want them to make after they have already chosen the alternative.

When you are learning about persuasion, it may seem easy. In reality, it is a strategy that requires a lot of time, effort, and practice. You cannot simply read about persuasion and then run out and master it. Instead, you really need to ensure that you grasp the concept and that you practice putting it into action in your daily life. In chapter 6 you will learn about many real-life strategies that can help you further integrate this technique into your life.

Manipulation

Manipulation tends to be regarded as one of the darker methods of mind control, and many people think it is a nasty thing to do. However, when you learn to use manipulation properly, you can use it to gain control over virtually anyone's mind and have your desired effect on their decisions and actions.

Unlike persuasion, which is typically comprised of conversational tactics, manipulation involves external influences to help encourage people to do what you want them to do. These include strategies like building trust, and proving why they should do what you want them to do. While some of these strategies are conversational, they are often impacted by external influences unlike persuasion which relies merely on wording structure and methods of structuring your sentences and conversations.

Deception

Deception is an extremely sophisticated strategy that is used in mind control. This is not the process of outright lying to people, but rather tactfully covering up certain pieces of information to avoid them from ever being discovered. This strategy allows people to knowingly omit information from conversations without being considered liars since they have never directly been asked, and therefore they have never directly lied.

When you are partaking in deception, you have to be tactful and consistent in keeping the conversation away from any question that may put you in a position where you must either come clean or actually lie. Using deception as a secondary manipulation method for mind control purposes means controlling the conversation and preventing it from ever going in the direction that would suggest information that you are lying or covering up information.

In order to skillfully use deception, you need to know how to guide the conversation in a way that leads the listener to believe something without ever actually being told to believe it. For example, if you want to prevent someone from finding out that you are attracted to someone they also like, you could create the illusion that you are not. You never actually admit that you aren't, you just lead the conversation so that it can be assumed that you aren't.

This is a powerful form of mind control because it allows you to deny ever doing anything wrong. Since you have never admitted to anything or lied about anything, you can easily say that it was the listeners fault for not asking, or for assuming anything was implied.

Subliminal Messages

When you use subliminal messages, you are sending messages without someone actually knowing that you are doing so. These messages tend to slip past the conscious mind and directly into the subconscious. The powerful thing about subliminal messages is that you can be telling someone one thing, and yet having them hear something entirely different. While this conscious mind digests something that they are willingly accepting, their subconscious mind may be hearing something entirely different. Because you have put them into a receptive mode, they are more likely to react and respond in the way that you want them to, and their subconscious mind is more likely to accept the information as well.

Subliminal messaging is powerful because it allows you to control the mind without any indication that you are doing so. You can speak directly through the conscious mind and into the subconscious mind, thus planting information, evidence, and knowledge into the subconscious that encourages your listener to support your position and act or think in the way that you want them to. You are literally programming their mind with your desired messages, and they have no idea that you are doing so.

Mind control is a very powerful strategy that can enable you to have people thinking in your favor. These individuals are going to unknowingly be listening extremely closely to your sentences and hanging on your every word, while giving into anything you want. Because of your masterful ability to control their minds without them even knowing it, you will be able to have any desired outcome effortlessly.

LEONARD MOORE

CHAPTER 2
MASTERFUL TECHNIQUES

Now that you are clear on the various types of mind control, you can start learning how you can master them! These techniques are all a part of the four primary mind control strategies you learned about in the previous chapter. Persuasion, manipulation, deception and subliminal messages are all strategies that are easily used by the average person, and can be used to achieve anything you desire in life with the help of anyone who you want to recruit.

Becoming clear on what each type of mind control is half the battle, because this will enable you to know when each strategy should be used. However, beyond that you need to know the exact techniques of each strategy. In this chapter, you are going to learn just that.

When you are reading this chapter, it may sound like a lot. There are many different techniques that are used by each strategy, so it can be overwhelming. The best thing you can do is take your time and learn each one, one at a time. Choose one area of focus and stay focused on that for about a week while you learn to naturally integrate it into your conversation and relationships. Then, you can move on to the next strategy. This may sound like it will take a long time, but it will also give you the opportunity to have the best results. If you attempt to go too fast, your techniques may have a forced feeling and that will take away from your success. Furthermore, it may cause your listener to know exactly what you are doing, which is not what you want. This chapter has been written in an ideal structure, where you can follow it one-at-a-time to get the best results. You don't need to choose one and then on to the other, simply follow the chapter chronologically and you will have the best results.

Persuasion Techniques

There are many ways to persuade people to think or behave in your favor. The following strategies are all methods of persuasion that you will want to master. Ideally, you will work on one or two at a time. If you try and rush it all, it may become extremely obvious as to what you are trying to do, and people may see through it. The goal is to practice something until you can seamlessly integrate it with your regular conversation so that no one even recognizes you are doing so. Over time, you can add in more and more, until you have completely mastered the art of persuasion.

Pacing

This ultimately means that you mirror someone else's behavior and language. When you can do so, you create a subconscious sense of connection between you and the individual you are talking to. You don't want to be extremely obvious when doing this, so don't entirely mirror them, but you want to do it enough that you create that subconscious message. If they touch their hair, you could fix yours. If you see that they are leaning to the left, wait a few moments and then naturally lean over to the left as well. When they say certain things, find a way to naturally work those words into the conversations so that they feel like you "get" them. This will help them feel connected to you and will assist them in establishing a sense of trust with you. When someone trusts you, they are much more likely to do what it is that you desire for them to do.

Pacing is the very first step of getting control in a conversation. When you pace, you give yourself the ability to subliminally tap into their subconscious and put them into a hypnotic state. They have no idea that you are doing so, so this is why it is considered such a powerful form of mind control. You will use this as your foundation to begin your brainwashing techniques.

Embedding

Once you have established the pacing part of the conversation, you can begin practicing embedding. This is the process whereby you embed certain commands into your conversations so that they begin to think in your favor. You are not directly telling them to do so, but because you are speaking into their subconscious mind you do hold an authority position where in suggesting it, you make them naturally *want* to do so.

Embedding commands into the conversation may seem difficult, but it is actually rather easy and it will have your listener deciding in your favor without you ever having to convince them to do so. You always want to make sure that you are embedding commands seamlessly so that they sound natural, and so that they don't sound like a command at all. You will learn about some real-life scenarios where this can be used in chapter 6, but one example you can consider right now would be if you were to want someone to take you on a date. Say you are having a conversation with them, you could say something such as "So, do you go on dates often?" by naturally working up to this phrase and then injecting it into the conversation, you give the listener the idea that they want to take you on a date. Then, they will make the decision without you ever having to outright ask or command it, or even have to make it seem like it was your idea to begin with.

Primary Motivators

Primary motivators are ultimately the reasons why someone would want to do what you are asking of them. There are many motivators, and you want to be certain that you structure them in the right way so that they motivate your listener and get the momentum building. By structuring your weaker and more powerful points properly, you can create an irreversible momentum that will get anyone working in your favor.

The best way to do this is to identify your primary motivators, and then identify your minor motivators. You want to use your primary motivators as the first and last part of motivation in your conversation, and then you want to inject the minor ones throughout the rest of the conversation. That way, the person you are talking to knows what the purpose of the conversation is from the beginning, and leaves the conversation with the purpose in mind as well. The fillers in the middle will all just provide extra information as to why they should make their decision in your favor.

Recent Knowledge

People are much more likely to stay focused on the last thing they heard in your conversation. While they will think about the fillers and everything in between, the pieces that will impact them most are the things they heard more recently. You can use this to your favor by sharing the most favorable information *after* the initial information so that they are more likely to pay attention to the favorable information versus the rest. This is a great way to take the attention away from the negative or lesser important parts of your conversation and keep people focused on the part you want them focused on.

Using this knowledge, you can bring the conversation back to where you want it to be at any given time. If the conversation is drawing away from the focus point or if anything negative or less desirable was shared, overshadow it with knowledge of the more favorable points so that they are more focused on the recent information. This will prevent them from working out of your favor by staying emphasized on the less desirable information instead of the more important information.

Repetition

There is a very high value that comes along with repetition. That is why advertisements are repeated everywhere, and why you can see them on many different platforms. That is why business people will give you a call back and do their best to regularly put their company name in front of your eyes. That is why when you hear about something several times, you are more interested in it and more likely to engage with it than you are if you only hear about it once. This is the same for your listener.

When you are having a conversation, repeat the same thing in various ways. Find new ways to present the information in a way that doesn't make you sound like a broken record, but helps your listener to stay focused on something. This idea is that they warm up to your information more and more each time, and eventually they are ready to decide in your favor.

You want to make sure that you make the repetition natural, and that you span it out over multiple conversations or interactions if necessary. This will ensure that this particular persuasion technique works and that the outcome is in your favor.

Anchoring

Anchoring is a very popular form of persuasion or mind control that uses physical action to talk to the subconscious mind. Anchoring is extremely easy in theory, but takes some practice in order to be able to do it in a way that actually works.

Essentially, anchoring works by "anchoring" one part of your body to "good" information, and one part to "bad" information. So, let's say you want to convince someone to travel to Spain instead of France. Anytime you talk about Spain you will naturally touch or point to one area on your body, let's say your left shoulder. However, anytime you talk about France you will touch or point to another area on your body, let's say the right hip. You want to make it very unobvious that you are doing this, so you don't want to clearly be pointing directly to this spot. Ideally, you will just casually gesture towards them and sometimes touch them. As a result, your listener will associate each area on your body with a certain point. They will see your left shoulder as "good" and your right hip as "bad". So, when you finally get to the punchline, if you say "So, where would you like to go?" while you are gesturing towards your left shoulder. As a result, their subconscious mind will be more likely to get their conscious mind to say Spain, because they have naturally associated your left shoulder with Spain which is "good".

These persuasion techniques are all types of conversational mannerisms you can use to have success with mind control. You want to use them during regular conversations as a method to structure your sentences and your general direction of conversation. You should take your time and really understand how each technique fits into your conversation so that you can work them in seamlessly. Having the control, tact, and technique to make the conversation flow naturally with these techniques planted inside of it will enable you to really use persuasion to its full effect. When you use persuasion properly, you will find that you no longer have to use obvious convincing as a method to persuade people to do what you want them to do. Instead, they will naturally be persuaded to listen to you because you have planted the idea in their mind throughout the conversation. Ultimately, they will think and act in your favor because you have implanted the idea to do so within the conversation. Instead of them thinking it was your idea and you pushed them into it, they will feel like it was their own idea and you were simply agreeing with them.

Manipulation Techniques

Being able to manipulate someone's thoughts is actually not as difficult as you may suspect, and it can have a powerful effect on your ability to get them to think in the way that you want them to think so that you can have your desired outcome.

There are seven ways that people can manipulate others. Unlike persuasion, these are not techniques that you use necessarily in conversation, such as anchoring or pacing. Rather, these are other important techniques that are involved in the relationship you build with the people you are talking to, and how you can use that relationship to manipulate them to have certain thoughts and decisions that work in your favor. The following strategies are an important part of manipulation.

Trust

Having the trust of the people you are talking to is important. When people trust you, they are much more likely to actually listen to you. They will feel more compelled to have conversations with you, they will be more likely to respect what you say, and they will be more likely to agree with you or comply with you when you exercise authority.

Gaining trust in your relationship comes from using tactics such as mirroring, as well as by generally being trustworthy. Show that you genuinely care about what they are saying, and that you have an interest in their wellbeing. Make them feel as though they can feel confident in your ability to think for their better interest so that they don't have to when they are with you. This way, when you make a request, suggestion, or subliminal command, they are much more likely to comply because they know you think with their best interest at heart.

Cause

You have to have cause when you are using any type of manipulation strategy. This means that you have a good reason why someone should do something. When you have a cause or reason why they would want to or should want to do anything, they are much more likely to actually want to do it. The incredible thing about manipulation and mindset is that you don't actually need to have an extremely great cause. As long as the cause is something that can be perceived as important and relevant, you can use it and it will work!

Secret Hypnosis

Secretly hypnotizing people without them knowing it is a powerful form of manipulation. Technically, you achieve this by using persuasion techniques such as pacing and anchoring. The reason why we mention this under the manipulation position is because it is important and relevant in both strategies. If you want to be able to successfully persuade and manipulate people to do what you want them to do, you need to be able to secretly hypnotize them. This is also relevant and important for deception and particularly subliminal messages.

When you have people under secret hypnosis, you can speak directly to their subconscious and you don't have to worry about their conscious mind getting in the way. While you do still need to accommodate for their conscious mind in the conversation, you have a direct passage to their subconscious mind to help activate your mind control strategies. It is important to understand how important this process is and activate it in every conversation when you want to be in control.

Using Irrelevant Tactics to Accomplish Relevant Goals

Perhaps you have heard of this technique before, but one of the best ways to get someone to say yes to what you actually want them to say yes to is to first get them to say yes to anything. Often, you want to start by getting them to say yes to things that are seemingly irrelevant to the overall picture. For example, if you want them to buy a TV you might first get them saying yes by asking them if they are interested in having a more luxurious living room or a more comfortable space for entertaining. That way you can then naturally draw them towards a TV and get them saying yes about larger sales.

You can also use this technique in many other areas. You can use it to get people to go on a date with you, to get them to go somewhere with you, to get them to give you things, or do any other number of things you might want them to do. This manipulation strategy really puts you in control and helps you get what you want. Soon, you will be able to get them to say yes to things that are unbelievably large.

Using Their Feelings

Arguing with logic can be hard because most people are driven by feelings, not logic. Even if they are highly logical people, they are more likely to be driven by logic *and* emotions, not merely logic. That is why getting into their emotional state and using their feelings to get desired results is often the best way to get what you want.

Proof of Results

People have always been more likely to act when there is proof that the results are what they are looking for. This is why having proof of the results they can expect when doing what you say will be extremely helpful in getting your way. Think about it this way: humans are herd animals; we do not like to be left behind or feel as though we are the odd one out. If you have proof that others have done it, then the people you are talking to are going to want to be one of those people, too. They will not want to be left out or feel as though they are the only ones not doing it, so they will naturally feel infinitely more inclined because they want to follow the herd.

Authority

People are naturally more inclined to comply to someone who speaks and acts with authority, instead of someone who appears to be intimidated or uncertain about what they are saying. If you are uncertain, waiver in your stance, or otherwise appear to be under confident, people are going to pick up on this and will feel less compelled to listen to you. They do not like to follow those who are not confident and strong. This could potentially lead them into a situation they don't want to be in. However, if you are leading with authority through confidence, strength, and certainty, people are going to assume that you know what you are talking about and they will feel more inclined to listen and comply.

Manipulation works heavily through knowing how to assert yourself in a conversation and use a human's nature against them. By understanding how people naturally behave, act, and think, you can use this to your advantage and create a situation that will allow you to carry the control in the conversation and manipulate people's thoughts and feelings to work in your favor.

Deception Techniques
Deception, as you know, is the process where you deceive someone instead of lie to them. In other words, you are knowingly omitting the truth and preventing someone from finding out through the way you guide the conversation. Deception in and of itself is a technique, though there are certain key points you can remember as an opportunity to maximize your deceptive abilities and have success with deception in conversation.

Avoid the Topic

The first and ultimately easiest way to exercise deception is to avoid the topic altogether. For example, if you do not want your boss to know that you weren't actually sick when you skipped work the other day, you would simply want to avoid the topic altogether. Without it ever coming up, you are never put into a situation where you have to actually use deception. This is a form of deception itself because you are allowing your boss to believe that you were truly sick, and you are omitting the truth from them. This is easy because you never have to actually use any of the other techniques with deception. You can simply rely on skirting the topic to allow your boss to continue believing that you were away sick, when in reality you were not sick at all but simply wanted or needed the day off for an alternative purpose.

Do Not Lie

Deception is different from lying in that you are not saying anything that isn't true. You are not telling something that is false, and therefore you are not lying. Instead, you are leading someone to believe false information through careful intention when you guide conversations. If you want to successfully deceive someone, you must refrain from lying at all costs. Lying puts the blame on you: the person can question why you were not truthful when you were asked something outright. However, when you deceive someone, the blame is on them. They were the ones who chose to believe without requiring further information, therefore they are the ones who are responsible for not having found out additional information. You can easily say "You never asked" when they ask why you never told them. This puts it on them, and away from you. They cannot blame you or generate a sense of mistrust based on the fact that you told an outright lie to them.

Careful Wording

Your wording is how you can avoid lying and instead use deception in conversation. You want to make sure that you carefully word things to lead someone to believe what you want them to believe, without actually lying to them to get them to believe it. For example, when you were calling for that sick day, you may have simply called in and said, "I need to take a sick day today." Nothing more, nothing less. Since you took a sick day, your boss will likely assume that you were actually sick. However, you never admitted to being sick, rather you simply stated that you needed to take a sick day. In other words, you were using your sick day as an opportunity to get the time off that you needed on that day.

The same goes for anything. You want to make sure that you are carefully wording your sentence to lead someone in one direction, without actually lying to get them there. Take your time, practice your wording, and look for loopholes that you can use to get people to believe you. This is how you can master deception.

Deceptive Actions

Deception can go much further than conversation and wording, as well. Deceptive actions can also assist you in achieving your desired result. This means that you act based on the truth you want them to believe, and not the realistic truth. For example, let's say you like your friend's spouse. Since you don't want them to find out, you can avoid the conversation and act as though you are merely friends with their spouse. You do not show that you are interested in them, you simply feel it and continue acting as regular friends with that person. You treat them the same as you would treat any other friend. This is deception through activity. You are not leading anyone to the truth, even though it exists. Instead, you are leading them in the other direction. You have never admitting to liking or not liking their spouse, it is simply assumed that you don't and your actions help lead people towards believing the same thing.

Subliminal Messages

Subliminal messages are a very powerful part of mind control, and are an extremely important strategy to learn if you want to successfully brainwash anyone. Subliminal messages are so powerful that they actually exist all over the modern world, and most of us don't even recognize it. They can be found in advertising, movies, news, and much more. Learning to use subliminal messages will help you successfully use mind control on people in the most masterful way. You will be able to brainwash anyone into thinking and behaving in the way that you desire for them to behave, and you will be able to have any outcome you desire once you master this technique. This is next level mind control that many people take years to master, but you are going to learn to master it easily and efficiently with these steps.

Scaling Back

This technique is an incredible way to use subliminal messaging to get people to do what you want them to do. Using this strategy will enable you to get people where you want them to be, easily. The technique is virtually effortless, and is often used in sales and other similar situations. You can modify it to work for anything, though. Essentially, all you need to do is start with a large request and scale it back as you are talking. For example, let's say you want to get someone to talk to you on the phone. You could start by asking to hang out and perhaps go on a date together. As the conversation progresses, however, work your way backwards and simply ask for a phone call. Because it is not as grandiose and intense as the original request, they are more likely to say yes. After all, a phone call seems to bear much less pressure than a request to go on a date, right? Then, once you have them on the phone you can push for the date!

First Name Basis

People absolutely love hearing their first names. It has a certain effect on people that is not achieved through virtually any other name in any language. Using someone's name is a sort of flattery that also validates someone's existence. People love knowing that they are recognized for the core of who they are, and they are much more likely to comply with what you are asking if you are using their first name regularly. You also want to refer them as what you want them to be for you. So, let's say you want "John" to become your friend. You could say "John, did you enjoy the game last night?" and when he says "Yeah, it was pretty good!" you could say "I agree, friend!" This associates them with being your friend, and is more likely to encourage them to actually feel as though they are your friend as well. This brings certain perks, such as trust, that are necessary to effectively use brainwashing and mind control, too.

Flattery

Many people argue that flattery will get you nowhere, but this is false. Flattery will get you everywhere if you use it right. People are attracted to those who are naturally charming and part of being charming is using flattery. If you take the time to charm those you are talking to, they are more likely to respond in your favor because you make them feel good. Something that is important to recognize with people, however, is the level of self-esteem they carry. Those who have high self-esteem will like to be flirted with heavily because you are validating their higher sense of self-esteem. Those who have low self-esteem, however, will become uncomfortable and intimidated if you flatter them too much. It causes them to feel as though they are being "buttered up" and makes them experience a conflict since they cannot relate to what you are saying. The more you practice identifying someone's sense of self-esteem, the easier it will be to gauge them and use this as an opportunity to flatter them in a way that will genuinely feel good to them and cause them to feel more inclined to respect your words and opinions.

One thing that is worth pointing out is that when you meet someone with extremely low self-esteem, you never want to go in the opposite direction and demean them. This will make them feel bad and break the trust between you two. If their self-esteem is phenomenally low, consider skipping this step altogether to prevent yourself from creating a disconnect between yourself and the person you are talking to.

Paraphrasing

People love to be validated, and paraphrasing is a great way to validate them. When you paraphrase someone, they feel as though you are listening to them carefully and that you are validating what they are saying. This makes them feel good, and develops a great sense of connection between the two of you. This is an excellent way to create that connection and use it as an opportunity to establish a trust between you and the person you are talking to, while also finding your way into their subconscious mind so that you can speak past their conscious mind and into their subconscious. This is how you will get maximum success with getting them to do what you want!

Nod A Lot

Nodding is connected with a positive agreeance between you and the person you are talking to. Nodding frequently throughout the conversation instills a very positive feeling into the person you are talking to, and helps them feel as though you are truly listening to them. When they see you nodding and agreeing with many parts of the conversation, they are going to feel more likely to nod and agree as well when it comes your turn to talk. This creates an overall positive situation where you can easily get them to agree with you, because the sense of "agreeance" is high in the conversation in general.

Repetition

One of the best ways that you can get through with subliminal messages is repetition. If you don't use repetition, your message is going to fall on deaf ears. The more you repeat certain words and phrases, the more the subconscious mind is going to hear it and you are going to have success with getting someone to agree with you and do what you want them to do. When you repeat something, it essentially "warms up" the mind to the idea, and helps people begin to really feel and believe it as the truth. The more you repeat it, the more they believe it and agree with it, and the more inclined they are to verbally agree with it in the real world, too. If you do not use repetition, you will never succeed in getting your messages and desires through to the person you are attempting to mind control.

Visual Subliminal Messages

Many people believe that audio messages are the only way to get subliminal messages through, but this is simply not true. In this day and age, we have access to text-based communications, and visually seeing the repetitive message can have a major impact on someone's likelihood of agreeing with you and making a positive connection with you and the message you are sharing. You can text your message to people without being overly obvious, and you can also find creative ways to share it on social media if you have them added. This will lead to them seeing the message beyond your conversations with them, which will even further warm their mind up to the idea and have them agreeing with you in no time.

Subliminal messages are a large part of brainwashing and mind control. These messages are generally thought to have little to no weight behind them, but they are intended to pack a punch and really leave a lasting impact on your listener without them even realizing it. To them, you may be innocently passing along a message, whereas to you, you are intentionally instilling this information into someone else's mind with ulterior motives of some sort.

Learning the techniques of mind control is not necessarily the easiest, and won't be an overnight process. It is important that you are prepared to practice these techniques over time, and that you are willing to allow yourself to expand your skills with practice. Brainwashing and mind control is a very powerful skill that you can learn, but you need to be extremely good at it if you are going to have the type of impact you want to have on people. You should refrain from trying to use too many of the techniques at once, because this will cause for you to become overwhelmed and will diminish the quality of your attempts. It may even lead people to seeing right through you and result in you having the opposite effect of what you are looking to accomplish.

The best way for you to master mind control is to work through this chapter slowly. Start at the very beginning and practice one or two techniques at a time. Make sure that you really give yourself time to master each one before you move onto the next one. You should aim to commit at least one week to each technique before it becomes habit and you are able to easily work it into conversations and use it naturally. Even if you don't necessarily want to get anything out of people, you should practice using these techniques in every conversation. Set small and easy goals with each conversation: perhaps to get someone to agree with you on an unpopular opinion, or to say something you want them to say without outright asking them to say it. Starting small like this will help you learn how each technique works, and warm yourself up to using it. In no time, you will be able to really get comfortable with these techniques and use them in larger scale operations, getting whatever you want whenever you want simply through the use of brainwashing and mind control techniques.

CHAPTER 3
THE ART OF NEVER GETTING CAUGHT

You cannot truly be a master of mind control if you find yourself getting caught when you are attempting to brainwash someone! If you want to have success, you need to know how to do things without getting caught. If you get caught, you will not only completely blow your chances at success in that conversation, but you could end up spoiling your reputation. People do not tend to take lightly to this type of situation, as no one likes the idea of being under mind control or brainwashed. In order to avoid this type of disaster, you need to know how to prevent yourself from getting caught. This chapter will teach you how to truly master mind control so that you are not at risk of being exposed and having your efforts destroyed by a blown cover.

Practice Regularly
The more you practice, the stronger your mind control game is going to become. You want to make sure that you practice often, preferably in every single conversation you have. Even if you don't actually want anything significant from someone, knowing how to get them to say or do certain things you want will help you practice brushing up on your technique. It could be something as

easy as getting someone to touch a certain area on their body, say something in particular, or do anything else small and seemingly unimportant. The more you learn to use these techniques to get what you want, the better.

When you practice regularly, the art of mind control becomes natural to your conversational mannerisms. You will stop having to actually think about the practice and will begin feeling confident in your natural abilities. Essentially, all of the techniques you practice will become a habit and you will simply use them, whether you intend to or not. You will be able to enter a conversation knowing what you want to get out of it, and you will be able to get it. Simple as that! If you do not practice regularly, it will always feel forced and you will feel pressured into making certain results which can eliminate the "natural" side of your efforts. This will diminish the quality of your results.

Take Your Time Expanding Your Skill

It cannot be stressed enough how important it is for you to slow down when it comes to practicing your skill. It may seem like a good idea to embrace many of these techniques at once and create a conversation that will help you get what you want, but this can lead to you being caught, quickly. When you put this type of pressure on yourself in a conversation without having any practice, you essentially infuse the conversation with a lot of unnatural and uncomfortable feeling. This is because you are not practiced at the techniques, so you are attempting to recall them and use them on the spot, and you are doing it with too many at once. People are going to see through you, and they are going to catch you in the act.

Instead, take your time. Learn one until the point that it genuinely feels natural for you to use it in conversation. You should be able to use it without having to think too much about it. This means that it has become natural to you and you are ready to move on to learning the next one. Once you have learned all of the techniques, you can continue practicing them all in your conversations and it should feel very natural. No one should be able to catch you because you are so natural and confident in these techniques.

Start Small

Sometimes, starting with large goals is honorable. When it comes to learning how to use mind control and not getting caught in the process, it is actually inefficient and an excellent way to get caught, quickly. The best thing you can do is start small with things that are seemingly unimportant and irrelevant. This allows you to practice getting people to say yes or do what you want them to do, with very little pressure on the situation overall. Once you get regular results in getting your smaller goals met, you can start practicing getting larger goals met. This will give you the best opportunity to really get natural in your talent and feel confident when it comes to setting out larger goals and accomplishing them.

Be Choosy About Who You Brainwash

It is very important that you are choosy about who you brainwash. Remember, just as you have the opportunity to learn about mind control, so do others. Many people in this day and age are somewhat knowledgeable about the art of mind control. While they may not be masters of it, they may have general knowledge around some tactics such as deceit and manipulation. It is important that you learn to identify those who are more likely to comply with your attempts and those who are more likely to be resistant against mind control.

As you practice with smaller goals, you will begin to identify trends in those who comply versus those who don't. It will become easier for you to identify those who are going to be more resistant against your strategies and those who are more likely to listen to you and do what you want. This will make it much easier for you to pick who you are going to use the strategies on. You want to make sure, obviously, that you are using them on the type of people who are more likely to comply. Those who aren't are more likely to catch you in the act and this could blow your cover.

Be Selective About Phrasing and Actions

It is very important that you are careful about the phrasing you use and the actions you carry when you are using mind control strategies. If you use the wrong phrasing, are too forceful or obvious in your phrasing, or have fidgety or otherwise uncontrolled physical movements, you are more likely to be caught. People will recognize that you have something "off" about you, and will be less likely to trust you or believe you. This means that you are going to ruin your attempts and even more people will be less likely to believe you, because mind control and manipulative types of reputations tend to be exposed and shared on a mass level to prevent other people from becoming manipulated. You need to be very careful in your actions and phrasing, ensuring that you are intentional and that you are behaving in a way that is not going to expose you and let others know what you are doing.

Getting caught can potentially destroy your success at mind control, as well as any relationships you have used this strategy in. When people catch wind that you are attempting to brainwash them, or that you have effectively done so, they will no longer trust you and this mistrust will spread across your network extremely quickly. People do not appreciate being subjected to brainwashing and mind control, and so they do not want to know that someone they have grown to trust is using it on them.

The absolute best strategy is to practice regularly and slowly, and be very picky about who you approach for larger requests. As you become more practiced, you may be able to approach a broader number of people, but in the meantime, you need to stick to only those who are going to be easy for you to brainwash. The more confident and practiced you become, the easier it will be for you to successfully get anything you want out of anyone you want. One bad experience, however, can not only diminish the trust of others but it can also eliminate your own confidence which will have a negative effect on your overall abilities. Take your time, develop confidence, and build up your practice slowly.

CHAPTER 4
SELF PROTECTION

In addition to knowing how to prevent yourself from getting caught, you need to know how you can prevent yourself from becoming subjected to brainwashing and mind control. After all, how can you truly be a master if someone can use your greatest weapon against you? This chapter will help ensure that you learn how to protect yourself against other people's brainwashing and mind control techniques. This will keep you in control of your own mind and ensure that you are always on top of your game.

Know the Strategies

When you know what it takes to brainwash someone, it becomes a lot easier to identify when those strategies are being used on yourself. The more you practice brainwashing others, the easier you are going to be able to identify these unique mannerisms in conversations with other people. This will be important when it comes to protecting yourself against being subjected to mind control. They always say that knowledge is the best prevention, and this is also true when it comes to brainwashing. The more you know, the better. If you are ever curious about whether or not you are being subjected to it, return to the technique chapter of this book and take a look through the most common and masterful techniques in mind control. This will help you identify whether or not someone was trying to brainwash you.

Don't Buy into Fear

Fear is one of the most popular strategies to manipulate someone into doing whatever you want them to do. It is used by a large majority of the government, media, and general society. This is one of the most popular strategies to get people to do what you want them to do. It has been used to get people to vote for certain government officials, like or dislike certain groups of people, and otherwise behave virtually however someone wants for them to behave.

When you notice scare tactics are being used, take the time to recognize it and do research to know whether or not what is being said holds any validity. This will help you know for sure whether or not you need to agree with the person attempting to brainwash you.

Fear works on the basis that it plays on people's emotions which, as you have learned, is one of the best ways to get people to agree with you. Instead of using logic, you simply use their emotions to get them to do what you want them to do. Make sure that you are not letting others use your emotions against you.

Learn to Consciously Recognize Subliminal Messaging

Subliminal messaging is everywhere in the modern world, and it is important that you do not allow yourself to be subjected to it. Not only is it present in mass media, mass advertising campaigns, and other major messages that are being shared with the world, but it also a part of other areas, too. Even entrepreneurs, independent marketers, and other people are using subliminal messages as an opportunity to get people to do what they want them to do. This is a common strategy that is being used by the average lay person, and it is important that you don't let this strategy be used against you.

Don't Follow the Herd

The herd tends to be guided by the mass media or government, which you have already learned tends to be responsible for brainwashing people. When you follow the herd, you are likely being brainwashed. This works on the basis of having proof: there is a proof that "everyone else is doing it" which might make you feel like you should do it, too. Remember that this is an extremely popular method of mind control, and it can be very easy to be subjected to. We often don't want to be the odd one out or left on the sidelines while everyone else does something, such as buy into trends or believe a certain common belief that may not actually be true to begin with. If you take the time to do research and pay attention to the realistic truth, you will refrain from being brainwashed by anyone else.

Stay in Control of Conversations

Do not let others control conversations with you. When they do, you are more likely to be subjected to brainwashing strategies that will actually have an effect on you. You don't necessarily need to be leading the conversation, but you need to be prepared to actually control the conversation. Part of that may be allowing the other person to believe they are in control when they actually aren't. In doing so, you can actually witness the strategies they are attempting to use and see how they might succeed and where they are failing. This will give you the opportunity to identify where you can do better with your own practice. If you allow others to control conversations and you don't consciously tune into this, you may end up finding that you become subjected to brainwashing strategies by others, which will result in you potentially agreeing to something you don't actually want to agree with.

Trust Your Instinct

When all else fails, trust your instinct. If you practice listening to it, you are more likely to know when someone is trying to brainwash you or get you to think, believe or do things that are not what you actually want to do. Your instinct can almost always identify when someone has ulterior motives and is attempting to get you to do something you don't actually want to. You may get a general feeling that something is wrong, or you may be able to identify exactly where they are trying to manipulate or control you. This will help you prevent yourself from getting brainwashed. You can then either take over the conversation and get into control over the situation, or simply exit the situation altogether.

Reflection

If you find that you have been brainwashed, you should take some time to reflect on the situation. Try and identify what happened that caused for the situation to be effective, and why you were able to be brainwashed. Look for the strategies that were used by the other person and how they were able to work on you. Make sure that you identify the opportunity to use this as a learning curve so that you can prevent yourself from being brainwashed in the future. You should also try and uncover the exact strategies they used so that you can learn a lesson or two from them. After all, if they were able to brainwash you, they must be pretty good at what they do! This means that you will be able to use their techniques going forward to enhance your own abilities and have greater success with mind control going forward.

Once you become a master at mind control yourself, it will be nearly impossible for anyone to use your strategy against you. Really, the only way they can is if they are better than you at your practice. This is why you should aim to become the best. You don't only want to be able to use it to get what you want, but you want to master it to avoid getting what you don't want. The more you practice mastering mind control, the more success you are going to have with it and the less likely you are going to be controlled by anyone else.

Remember, knowledge is the best tool for prevention. If you really want to prevent yourself from becoming brainwashed by anyone else, arm yourself with knowledge of the various methods they could use to brainwash you so that you are less likely to be effected by it.

Additionally, if you find that you ever have been brainwashed, always look at it as an opportunity to learn more about the art. This will give you the chance to master your practice even more, and eventually become the most masterful mind control artist that exists. You will not be able to be brainwashed by anyone once you are fully aware of what it looks like and feels like to be under mind control. This will also step up your own practice because you will be able to enforce the techniques of others in order to have total success with your own practice.

It is important that you always work towards learning how to prevent yourself from becoming subjected to mind control. You never want your own practice to be used against you, as this will really cripple your confidence and take away from your own success with mind control. Mistakes are bound to happen, but you always want to be aiming higher. Otherwise, you will never be able to have total success in getting your way and having success with mind control because you will be continually under the control of others. This is ineffective and will destroy your success. Do not let this happen.

CHAPTER 5
USING MIND CONTROL
IN REAL LIFE

Learning about mind control is most effective when you get an idea of what it truly looks like in action. This will ensure that you are right in your beliefs about how each technique should look, and that you are prepared to use it in your own real-life scenarios. The following three sample scenarios will teach you exactly what mind control strategies should look like in action when you are using them. This will help you get an idea of what it should truly look like when you are masterful at using mind control on people.

Scenario One: Make a Sale

One situation where you may want to exercise your brainwashing abilities is to make a sale in your business. With the modern world being taken over by entrepreneurs, it can be easy to feel like you might be one of the few who struggles with sales. You can certainly change the face of this experience by learning how to use brainwashing to get people to purchase products from you.

Imagine the following scenario between Margaret (the

buyer) and Darren (the seller). This will help you get an idea of what mind control would look like in real life in this particular situation.

Margaret: "What an interesting product. I don't know how I would ever use it, but it's definitely interesting!"

Darren: "Thanks! This is a state of the art potato masher. I know it may look intimidating, but it is actually in incredible piece!"

Margaret: "A potato masher? I would have never guessed; it looks so high tech! What would you ever need such a fancy piece for? I've had the same one for years and it works just fine."

Darren: "Funny you should ask! What was your name again, friend?"

Margaret: "Margaret!"

Darren: "Well, Margaret, that is a beautiful name! This state of the art potato masher, is an incredible piece that enables you to mash your potatoes into a creamy blend. You can also use it to rice your potatoes, which is a neat ability that I bet your potato masher can't do!"

Margaret: "No, it certainly can't!"

Darren: "One thing I love about this phenomenal potato masher is that it allows me to achieve a creamy texture that my old one couldn't. Plus, I don't have to put in any extra energy! In fact, it's easier! I get to enjoy extra potatoes *and* my arm doesn't hurt from mashing the entire pot!"

Margaret: "Oh! Yes, I certainly know what it is like to get the sore arm. You know, I find that to be troublesome and I actually don't make potatoes often because of it. But still, it seems so much fancier! I don't even know how you would use it!"

Darren: "Here, Margaret, let me show you! See how it mashes this potato down so easily? My Mom loves this device because it makes the process so much easier. She says when we're having family dinner she can still make my Dad's favorite rosemary and garlic mashed potatoes without having her arthritis act up in her wrist!"

Margaret: "Is that so? Wow!"

Darren: "Why don't you give it a try?"

Margaret: "Sure!"

Darren: "What do you think, Margaret?"

Margaret: "Well, it is certainly incredible! I could see myself using this. What would a piece like this cost me?"

Darren: "Margaret, it is your lucky day! This potato masher regularly costs $59.95, but today they went on sale for just $39.99!"

Margaret: "Oh my! $40 for a potato masher? That is a lot of money!"

Darren: "Well, Margaret, the thing about this incredible potato masher is that you are not only getting the masher, but the ricer. Also, it comes with this extremely soft grip handle to ensure that it is easy for absolutely anyone to use! That means that when you replace your old one with it, you will be certain to keep this one for many years, too! Plus, it has a lifetime warranty!"

Margaret: "I'll take one!"

In the above scenario, Darren learned Margaret's name and used charm to help her feel comfortable with him. He also ensured that he regularly talked about how incredible the potato masher was. When Margaret rose concerns that the potato masher was expensive, he used proof to explain why it was such an awesome piece, and repeated the value she was getting in a few unique ways before allowing her to make the decision. You can also see where deceit was used, as Darren did not discuss the price until after Margaret had already used the product and admitted that she liked it.

These techniques were worked naturally into the conversation, and enabled Darren to lead the conversation. Margaret showed up at the supermarket that day with no intention of leaving with a new potato masher, and Darren began his conversation with Margaret with no intention of letting her leave without one. He did not push it onto her or at any time make her feel as though she was being pressured into the sale. Instead, he used repetition, proof, and feelings to help her see why she needed the potato masher so badly. This allowed him to make the sale in a way that did not in any way suggest that he was brainwashing Margaret into believing that she truly needed the potato masher.

Scenario Two: Going on a Date

Getting someone to go on a date with you can sometimes be difficult. Many times, we may pull back or even avoid asking anyone out because we fear rejection. Luckily, mind control techniques can be used to not only help you build your confidence, but also land you the date you want to go on.

The following scenario is one between Jason (the asker) and Louise (the one who wanted to be asked.) See if you can identify the areas where mind control is used before we even begin discussing that portion at the end of the conversation.

Jason: "Hey, Louise! Long time no see. How is my old pal doing?"

Louise: "Hey, Jason, I'm good thanks. Just went out an incredible date last night with this guy from work. We probably won't do it again, but I had a lot of fun anyway!"

Jason: "That sounds great! What did you guys do?"

Louise: "Well, he took me to laser tag, which seems very juvenile! I was hoping he would take me to dinner and show me his mature side, but he never did. Guys can be like that, you know?"

Jason: "I guess!"

Louise: "Well what did you do the last time you took a girl on a date, Jason?"

Jason: "We went out to eat at a local lobster restaurant! The drinks there were killer, have you ever been?"

Louise: "I haven't! It sounds amazing. Maybe one day someone will treat me to a date like that!"

Jason: "Maybe!"

Louise: "Speaking of lobster, it has been so long since I've had any. I wonder who would want to go with me!"

Jason: "Why don't you and I go together? I'll treat you to the date you are looking for!"

Louise: "Oh! Sure!"

In this short conversation, Louise brings up the fact that she wants to go on a date, but is disappointed that men are always immature when she agrees to go on them. She has fun, but doesn't see the relationship going anywhere because she wants someone who is mature. Jason admits that he takes his dates on mature dates to places such as the local lobster restaurant. Louise wants to go on a date with Jason, and experience what it would be like to date someone who is mature and can hold a conversation with someone through dinner. She continues to talk about dates and bring up the fact that she would love to go on one. When Jason talks about lobster, Louise paraphrases his conversation by speaking about lobster and how much she would enjoy a date like that. Jason then asks Louise out for a date. Louise planted the idea of going on a date together all along, but allowed Jason to feel as though he was the one responsible for coming up with the idea. She used deceit to make it seem as though she was planning on asking someone else to go, when in reality she was wanting Jason to ask her.

Scenario Three: Getting a Promotion

Getting a promotion may seem difficult, but when you are a master at brainwashing it can be extremely easy. In the following scenario, you will learn about how Linda (the employee) brainwashes George (the boss) into giving her a promotion at her job.

George: "Linda, do you know why I have called you into my office today?"

Linda: "It is my two-year review, right?"

George: "That's right Linda! I want to talk about how you are doing in your job recently. Would you like to share your thoughts with me?"

Linda: "Well, George, I really think I have been doing well! Recently Susanne got laid off, so I have had to pick up a lot of the slack with her being gone. I have been handling it well though! Terri, our supervisor, seems to be unaware of how much of a struggle this can be, though. I often find everyone coming to me for help because he simply doesn't understand what needs to be done!"

George: "It sounds like you have been taking on a lot of extra responsibility lately. I have seen you taking part in a lot more activities at work lately, too, which I like."

Linda: "Yes! Well, you know I'm coming after your job, George! One day I'm going to run this show"

George: "Ha-ha, I won't be leaving any time soon!"

Linda: "Well, good! I still have more to learn from you. I do wish I could have more responsibility, though. With everyone coming to me for help, I feel as though I could assist them more if I had more authority on the floor. If a position like Terri's ever opened up, I would really like to be considered for it, please!"

George: "Well, Linda, I will keep that in mind! In the meantime, let's discuss your sales. How have your numbers been?"

Linda: "Oh they have been incredible! I have been really feeling confident in my ability to help customers find what they are looking for and get the products that serve their needs. This truly is such an amazing job. I look forward to coming to work every day, and am grateful to have found a company where I can stay for a long time! I also appreciate the opportunity to grow into more advanced positions over time!"

George: "That sounds amazing, Linda! I'm happy you are feeling so confident in your position. Look, I don't have any supervisor roles available right now, but I do have a sales lead position. What do you say we put you in that position and start training you to take over the next supervisor role that becomes available? It will come with the added responsibility you desire, and a raise to compensate you for the extra work you will be doing around here!"

Linda: "Wow, thank you so much George! I really appreciate it!"

You can see how easily Linda led this conversation the entire time. She always answered George's questions, but was able to turn the answers around to repeat that she wanted to be promoted to a higher position within the company. She started by saying that she wanted to go for George's position as a manager, but then scaled back to say that she only wanted to be put in the supervisor position. This ensured George didn't feel threatened by her intentions, and also proved that she wanted more within' the business. She also used his name regularly, as we know this is a powerful method of somewhat seducing someone into feeling trustworthy and comfortable around you. Linda also used proof to show that she was already doing incredible in her position and that she was shouldering many responsibilities above her current level. This proved that she was capable of meeting the needs of the company. As a result, George wanted to compensate her for her hard work and ensure that she wanted to remain faithful to the company, as she expressed that she already was. This is how you can easily use mind control to get a promotion at work!

The above situations are excellent real-life scenarios that help show you exactly how natural and effortless mind control strategies are once you have practiced them. In each conversation, the brainwasher was entirely in control and knew exactly what to say in order to get the other person to do what they wanted them to do. Everything was natural and comfortable, and nothing was forced.

The biggest strategy of repetition was used throughout every conversation and you can see how it contributed to helping the listener foster the opinion of the person leading the conversation. This is a powerful tool, and should never be overlooked. This is essentially the way that you can change someone's mind, without ever having to convince them to believe something new.

When you master the art of mind control, you will find that these scenarios are exactly what your own natural abilities will begin to represent. You will be able to have very natural conversations that flow smoothly, and yet still get you the exact results you desire. Everything else will come easily because you have mastered the art of brainwashing. Remember, it takes time but it can be this easy for you, too!

CONCLUSION

Thank you for reading *Mind Control: Forbidden Manipulation and Deception Techniques to Persuade and Brainwash Anyone.*

This guidebook was written as an effort to teach you all about mind control and how you can master this technique in your life. When you employ the skills of manipulation, deception, persuasion and subliminal messages, you put yourself in a position where you can completely control your life and have any outcome you desire. You no longer have to use convincing, begging, pleading, nagging, or other forceful methods to try, and probably fail, at getting your way. Instead, you can get literally anything you want using these techniques. Whether you want money, a sale, a date, someone to leave you alone, or any other number of things, you can get them using these techniques.

I hope you were able to learn about the power of mind control and how you can use it to lead the life you desire. While you could simply wait and gamble on luck and faith, you could also take matters into your own hands and design your dream life. Brainwashing people is the easiest way to get what you want, when you want it. I hope this book was able to teach you about the techniques of manipulation, deception, persuasion, subliminal messages, and other mind control strategies to help you design your own life.

I hope you were also able to learn about how you can prevent yourself from getting caught, and from being brainwashed by someone else. Remember, a lot of the prevention comes from being educated and taking your time. Make sure that you are well practiced before you unleash your skills on just anybody, and always start small to ensure that you are confident and skilled enough to get the outcomes you desire without being caught.

The next step is to begin practicing all of the tools you have been provided with, and using them as an opportunity to change your life. Beginning right now in this very moment, you no longer have to rely on others to help you get the life you desire. Instead, you can create it on your own using mind control to get there. Anything you want is at your beck and call. Simply make sure that you have practiced so that you can truly get what you want without straying away from brainwashing and ultimately forcing people into giving you what you want. This is an easy way to get caught and diminish your success at getting what you want.

Lastly, if you enjoyed this book I ask that you please take the time to leave your honest feedback on Amazon Kindle. Your review would be greatly appreciated.

Thank you, and best of luck!

Printed in Great Britain
by Amazon